BABY LOOPS & TWISTS

LEISURE ARTS, INC. Maumelle, Arkansas

Introduction

Loop yarn is the perfect yarn to create baby accessories. It is a special yarn that comes with stitches already made and is the perfect craft yarn to finger knit for kids and adults. This yarn removes the necessity to use knitting needles or crochet hooks, and even those who don't know how to knit can easily learn how to knit with this yarn. No more excuses such as "I can't knit or crochet," because with this yarn, anybody can and will be able to knit. It's the ultimate finger knitting yarn!

This book will use different techniques to create a variety of baby items that you can use or gift. Most of the items will make up quickly, and are so soft for any baby! If you still need assistance, there are videos to guide you through, too! Kristi Simpson demonstrates each stitch used in this book, helpful tips for each item and many helpful tips and tricks on her website: www.KristiSimpson.net. Feel free to use those videos to learn, teach and complete each project in this book.

Now, grab that fluffy, soft, loopy yarn
and let's get started!

Basket

 **BASIC**

You can never have too many baskets when storing baby items. Grab one skein each of two colors to create this cute storage basket. It uses just the basic stitches to complete and you'll also learn how to add those cute ruffles on the edge!

Approximate Finished Size:
10" square x 4½" deep (25.5 cm x 11.5 cm)

SHOPPING LIST

Yarn (Jumbo Weight) **7**
[6.4 ounces, 18 yards
(180 grams, 16 meters) per skein]:
☐ Variegated - 1 skein
☐ Mauve - 1 skein

Additional Supplies
☐ Scissors
☐ Large eye tapestry
  or yarn needle

*Please review General Instructions,
pages 52-63, before beginning Basket.*

TECHNIQUE USED

KNIT 2 STITCHES TOGETHER (uses next 2 stitches)
Cross the next 2 stitches as indicated (**right over left** *OR* **left over right**), then pass the next loop from the working yarn through the two stitches from **back** to **front**, knitting them together as if they were one stitch (**one stitch made**).

INSTRUCTIONS

BOTTOM

To begin, open the first loop of Variegated by cutting the center to create a longer length for weaving in the end.

Cast on 13 loops.

Row 1: Working from **right** to **left**, knit each stitch across.

Row 2: Working from **left** to **right**, knit each stitch across.

Rows 3-12: Repeat Rows 1 and 2, 5 times.

Cut Variegated 3 loops **past** the last stitch. Cut the loops open so you will have a long tail.

Bind off all stitches from **left** to **right**.

Bring the long tail from **back** to **front** through the remaining stitch.

SIDES

Open the first loop of Variegated to create a long end.

Working from **right** to **left**, pull up 13 loops across bound off edge; pull up a loop in end of each row across; pull up 13 loops across cast on edge; pull up a loop in end of each row across: 50 stitches.

Rounds 1-4: Working from **right** to **left (now and throughout)**, knit each stitch around.

Round 5: Knit the first 6 stitches, knit 2 stitches together, ★ knit the next 4 stitches, knit 2 stitches together; repeat from ★ around: 42 stitches.

Round 6: Knit each stitch around; cut Variegated 2 loops **past** the last stitch. Cut the last loop open so you will have a long tail (first loop will be used to bind off on Round 8).

Round 7 (Decorative round)**:** With Mauve in **back** of work, ★ insert the next Variegated stitch from **front** to **back** through the next Mauve loop of the working yarn (Mauve loops will be toward you); repeat from ★ around.

Cut Mauve one loop **past** the last stitch. Cut the loop open so you will have a long tail.

Round 8: Beginning with the Variegated loop left at end of Round 6, bind off each stitch around; bring the Variegated tail from **back** to **front** under both loops of the first stitch of the round, **then** down through the center of the remaining stitch.

Thread your yarn or tapestry needle with the long ends and weave them back and forth through the back of the stitches.

Blanket

 **BASIC**

Wow all of your friends and family with this stunning blanket. Do not be intimidated by the 'fancy' design! If you can count loops you can do this! The blanket has a purl center so that the cabled border pops out.

Approximate Finished Size:
34" wide x 33" long (86.5 cm x 84 cm)

SHOPPING LIST

Yarn (Jumbo Weight) **JUMBO 7**
[6.4 ounces, 18 yards
(180 grams, 16 meters) per skein]:
☐ 3 skeins

Additional Supplies
☐ Scissors
☐ Large tapestry or yarn needle

Please review General Instructions, pages 52-63, before beginning Blanket.

TECHNIQUES USED

CABLE 2 LEFT *(abbreviated C2L)* (uses next 2 stitches)
Cross the **next** stitch to the **left** in **front** of the following stitch, then knit the stitches in working order.
CABLE 2 RIGHT *(abbreviated C2R)* (uses next 2 stitches)
Cross the **next** stitch to the **right** in **front** of the following stitch, then knit the stitches in working order.

INSTRUCTIONS

To begin, open the first loop by cutting the center to create a longer length for weaving in the end.

Cast on 50 loops.

Row 1: Working from **right** to **left**, knit the first stitch, work C2L across to the last stitch, knit the last stitch.

Row 2: Working from **left** to **right**, work C2R across.

Rows 3-6: Repeat Rows 1 and 2 twice.

Row 7: Working from **right** to **left**, knit the first stitch, work C2L 3 times, purl the next 36 stitches, work C2L 3 times, knit the last stitch.

Row 8: Working from **left** to **right**, work C2R 4 times, purl the next 34 stitches, work C2R 4 times.

Rows 9-34: Repeat Rows 7 and 8, 13 times.

Row 35: Working from **right** to **left**, knit the first stitch, work C2L across to the last stitch, knit the last stitch.

Row 36: Working from **left** to **right**, work C2R across.

Rows 37-40: Repeat Rows 35 and 36 twice.

Bind off all stitches from **left** to **right**.

Thread your yarn or tapestry needle with the long ends and weave them back and forth through the back of the stitches.

Burp Cloth

 BASIC

This burp cloth is made with the baby and mom in mind. It is super soft for the baby and contoured for the mom. Just throw it over your shoulder and snuggle away. The stitches in this pattern are the knit and knit 2 together with a finishing trim that's easy to complete.

Approximate Finished Measurements:
11" wide x 25" long (28 cm x 63.5 cm)

SHOPPING LIST

Yarn (Jumbo Weight)
[6.4 ounces, 18 yards
(180 grams, 16 meters) per skein]:
☐ Grey - 1 skein
☐ Mauve - 1 skein

Additional Supplies
☐ Scissors
☐ Large eye tapestry or yarn needle

Please review General Instructions,
pages 52-63, before beginning Burp Cloth.

TECHNIQUES USED

INCREASE (uses one stitch)
With the yarn in the **back**, pass the next 2 loops from the working yarn from **back** to **front** through the stitch indicated **(2 stitches made)**.

KNIT 2 STITCHES TOGETHER (uses next 2 stitches)
Cross the next 2 stitches as indicated **(right over left OR left over right)**, then pass the next loop from the working yarn through the two stitches from **back** to **front**, knitting them together as if they were one stitch **(one stitch made)**.

INSTRUCTIONS

BODY

To begin, open the first loop of Grey by cutting the center to create a longer length for weaving in the end.

Cast on 8 loops.

Row 1: Working from **right** to **left**, increase in the first stitch, knit the next 6 stitches, increase in the last stitch: 10 stitches.

Row 2: Working from **left** to **right**, knit each stitch across.

Row 3 (Increase row)**:** Working from **right** to **left**, increase in the first stitch, knit each stitch across to the last stitch, increase in the last stitch: 12 stitches.

Rows 4-7: Repeat Rows 2 and 3 twice: 16 stitches.

Row 8: Working from **left** to **right**, knit each stitch across.

Row 9: Working from **right** to **left**, knit each stitch across.

Row 10: Working from **left** to **right,** knit each stitch across.

Row 11 (Decrease row)**:** Working from **right** to **left**, knit the first 2 stitches together (**right over left**), knit each stitch across to the last 2 stitches, knit the last 2 stitches together (**left over right**): 14 stitches.

Row 12 (Decrease row)**:** Working from **left** to **right**, knit the first 2 stitches together (**left over right**), knit each stitch across to the last 2 stitches, knit the last 2 stitches together (**right over left**): 12 stitches.

Rows 13 and 14: Repeat Rows 11 and 12: 8 stitches.

Rows 15-21: Repeat Rows 1-7: 16 stitches.

Row 22 (Decrease row): Working from **left** to **right**, knit the first 2 stitches together **(left over right)**, knit each stitch across to the last 2 stitches, knit the last 2 stitches together **(right over left)**: 14 stitches.

Row 23: Working from **right** to **left,** knit each stitch across.

Rows 24-28: Repeat Rows 22 and 23 twice, then repeat Row 22 once **more**: 8 stitches.

Bind off all stitches from **left** to **right**.

TRIM

To begin, open the first loop of Mauve by cutting the center to create a longer length for weaving in the end.

With the same side of the Body facing and working from **right** to **left**, pull up 2 loops in the first bound off stitch, pull up a loop in each stitch across to the last stitch, pull up 2 loops in the last stitch; working in the end of rows, (pull up a loop in the next row, pull up 2 loops in the next row) 4 times, pull up a loop in each of the next 10 rows, (pull up 2 loops in the next row, pull up a loop in the next row) 4 times; working across the cast on edge, pull up 2 loops in the first stitch, pull up a loop in each stitch across to the last stitch, pull up 2 loops in last stitch; working in the end of rows, (pull up a loop in the next row, pull up 2 loops in the next row) 4 times, pull up a loop in each of next 10 rows, (pull up 2 loops in the next row, pull up a loop in the next row) 4 times.

Beginning with the next unworked loop from the working yarn, bind off all stitches from **right** to **left**.

Cut Mauve 3 loops **past** the last stitch. Cut the loops open so you will have a long tail.

Bring the long tail from **back** to **front** under both loops of the first stitch of the round, **then** down through the center of the remaining stitch.

Thread your yarn or tapestry needle with the long ends and weave them back and forth through the back of the stitches.

Diaper Case

 **BASIC**

Take an everyday necessity and make it fashionable with the chevron stitch! This clutch can be made with any 2 colors and you only need one skein of each color to complete. Believe it or not, you'll use the same one row to complete the entire project.

Approximate Finished Size:
11" wide x 33" long (28 cm x 84 cm)
(laying flat and measured thru the center of the length)

SHOPPING LIST

Yarn (Jumbo Weight) 🧶**7**
[6.4 ounces, 18 yards
(180 grams, 16 meters) per skein]:
☐ Mauve - 1 skein
☐ Grey - 1 skein

Additional Supplies
☐ Scissors
☐ Large eye tapestry or yarn needle

*Please review General Instructions,
pages 52-63, before beginning Diaper Case.*

TECHNIQUES USED

INCREASE (uses one stitch)
With the yarn in the **back**, pass the next 2 loops from the working yarn from **back** to **front** through the stitch indicated **(2 stitches made)**.
KNIT 3 STITCHES TOGETHER (uses next 3 stitches)
Hold the next stitch **behind** the second stitch and the third stitch **behind** the first stitch, then pass the next loop from the working yarn through all 3 stitches from **back** to **front**, knitting them together as if they were one stitch **(one stitch made)**.

INSTRUCTIONS

To begin, open the first 4 loops of Mauve by cutting the centers to create a longer length for sewing and weaving.

Cast on 19 loops.

Row 1: Working from **right** to **left**, increase in the first stitch, knit the next 7 stitches, knit 3 stitches together, knit the next 7 stitches, increase in the last stitch: 19 stitches.

Note: When changing colors at the end of a row, cut the yarn 4 loops **past** the last stitch to create a longer length for sewing and weaving.

Row 2: Working from **left** to **right**, increase in the first stitch, knit the next 7 stitches, knit 3 stitches together, knit the next 7 stitches, increase in the last stitch; cut Mauve and change to Grey.

Row 3: With Grey and working from **right** to **left**, increase in the first stitch, knit the next 7 stitches, knit 3 stitches together, knit the next 7 stitches, increase in the last stitch.

Row 4: Working from **left** to **right**, increase in the first stitch, knit the next 7 stitches, knit 3 stitches together, knit the next 7 stitches, increase in the last stitch.

Row 5: Working from **right** to **left**, increase in the first stitch, knit the next 7 stitches, knit 3 stitches together, knit the next 7 stitches, increase in the last stitch; cut Grey and change to Mauve.

Row 6: With Mauve and working from **left** to **right**, increase in the first stitch, knit the next 7 stitches, knit 3 stitches together, knit the next 7 stitches, increase in the last stitch.

Row 7: Working from **right** to **left**, increase in the first stitch, knit the next 7 stitches, knit 3 stitches together, knit the next 7 stitches, increase in the last stitch.

Row 8: Working from **left** to **right**, increase in the first stitch, knit the next 7 stitches, knit 3 stitches together, knit the next 7 stitches, increase in the last stitch; cut Mauve and change to Grey.

Rows 9-29: Repeat Rows 3-8, 3 times; then repeat Rows 3-5 once **more**; at the end of Row 29, do **not** cut Grey or change to Mauve.

Row 30: Continuing with Grey and working from **left** to **right**, knit the first 8 stitches, knit 3 stitches together, knit the last 8 stitches: 17 stitches.

Bind off all stitches from **left** to **right**.

Cut Grey 4 loops **past** the last stitch. Cut the loops open so you will have a long tail.

Fold in the ends, matching stripes and leaving approximately 5-6" (12.5-15 cm) in center for folding.

Sew the end of the rows together on each side, then weave the ends back and forth through the back of the stitches.

Hat

 **BASIC**

Every baby needs a soft and warm hat...and this yarn will make several hats per skein! It's so fast and easy, you'll have a stash made before you know it! You'll use the basic stitches in this pattern: cast on, knit, purl and bind off.

SHOPPING LIST

Yarn (Jumbo Weight) **JUMBO 7**
[6.4 ounces, 18 yards
(180 grams, 16 meters) per skein]:
☐ 1 skein will make **both** sizes
of Hat

Additional Supplies
☐ Split-ring marker
☐ Scissors
☐ Large eye tapestry or yarn needle

*Please review General Instructions,
pages 52-63, before beginning Hat.*

SIZE INFORMATION

Fits up to 15{17}"/38{43} cm Head circumference

Size Note: We have printed the instructions for the sizes in different colors to make it easier for you to find:

- size Small in Blue
- size Medium in Pink

Instructions in Black apply to both sizes.

TECHNIQUE USED

INCREASE (uses one stitch)

With the yarn in the **back**, pass the next 2 loops from the working yarn from **back** to **front** through the stitch indicated (**2 stitches made**).

INSTRUCTIONS

To begin, open the first two loops by cutting the centers to create a longer length for tying and weaving in the end.

Cast on 4 loops. Tie a knot after the 4th loop to create a ring (between the 4th and 5th loops). **(SEE PHOTO BELOW)**

Round 1 (Increase round)**:** Working from **right** to **left (now and throughout)**, increase in each stitch around: 8 stitches.

Note: Place a split-ring marker around the first stitch of each round to indicate the beginning of the round. Move the marker at the beginning of each round. Remove the marker when it's no longer needed.

Round 2: ★ Knit the next stitch, increase in the next stitch; repeat from ★ around: 12 stitches.

Round 3: ★ Knit the next 2 stitches, increase in the next stitch; repeat from ★ around: 16 stitches.

Round 4: ★ Knit the next 3 stitches, increase in the next stitch; repeat from ★ around: 20 stitches.

Size Medium ONLY
Round 5: ★ Knit the next 4 stitches, increase in the next stitch; repeat from ★ around: 24 stitches.

Both Sizes
Next 2 Rounds: Knit each stitch around.

Last 2 Rounds: Working from **right** to **left** with the yarn in the **front**, purl each stitch around.

Cut the yarn 3 loops **past** the last stitch. Cut the loops open so you will have a long tail.

Working from **right** to **left**, with long tail at **wrong** side and beginning with the last stitch of the last round, bind off all stitches.

Bring the long tail from **back** to **front** under both loops of the first stitch of the round, **then** down through the center of the remaining stitch.

Thread your yarn or tapestry needle with the long ends and weave them back and forth through the back of the stitches.

Leg Warmers

Keep those baby legs warmer in this sweet set of legwarmers. The pattern is only 9 rows, so it's not only fast— but adorable! By mixing knit and purl stitches, you will get a fantastic pattern that looks hard, but is super easy!

Approximate Finished Size:
Fits 3-6 months

SHOPPING LIST

Yarn (Jumbo Weight) 🧶**7**
[6.4 ounces, 18 yards
(180 grams, 16 meters) per skein]:
☐ 1 skein

Additional Supplies
☐ Scissors
☐ Large eye tapestry
  or yarn needle

Please review General Instructions, pages 52-63, before beginning Leg Warmers.

INSTRUCTIONS

To begin, open the first loop by cutting the center to create a longer length for weaving in the end.

Cast on 10 loops.

Row 1: Working from **right** to **left** with the yarn in the **front**, purl the first 2 stitches, knit the next 6 stitches, purl the last 2 stitches.

Row 2: Working from **left** to **right**, purl the first 2 stitches, knit the next 6 stitches, purl the last 2 stitches.

Row 3: Working from **right** to **left**, purl the first 2 stitches, knit the next 6 stitches, purl the last 2 stitches.

Rows 4-9: Repeat Rows 2 and 3, 3 times.

Cut the yarn 3 loops **past** the last stitch. Open the loops by cutting the centers to create a longer length for weaving in the end.

Joining: Bring cast on edge up to meet the stitches on Row 9 so the **wrong** side is together. Pull each stitch of Row 9 through the base of the cast on stitches. Then, working from **left** to **right**, bind off all stitches.

Bring the long tail through the remaining stitch.

Thread your yarn or tapestry needle with the long ends and weave them back and forth through the back of the stitches.

Repeat for second Leg Warmer.

Penguin Pillow

■□□□ **BASIC**

This yarn is so much fun to get creative with. This penguin pillow uses the basic stitches and then we finish with the cutest webbed feet! It's fun to see this pillow come together, so let's get started.

Approximate Finished Size:
14" wide x 15" tall (35.5 cm x 38 cm)

SHOPPING LIST

Yarn (Jumbo Weight) 🧶**7** JUMBO
[6.4 ounces, 18 yards
(180 grams, 16 meters) per skein]:
☐ Black - 1 skein
☐ Cream - 1 skein
☐ Orange - 1 skein

Additional Supplies
☐ Split-ring marker
☐ Scissors
☐ Polyester fiberfill
☐ Large eye tapestry or yarn needle

*Please review General Instructions,
pages 52-63, before beginning Pillow.*

TECHNIQUES USED

INCREASE (uses one stitch)

With the yarn in the **back**, pass the next 2 loops from the working yarn from **back** to **front** through the stitch indicated (**2 stitches made**).

KNIT 2 STITCHES TOGETHER (uses next 2 stitches)

Cross the next 2 stitches as indicated (**right over left** *OR* **left over right**), then pass the next loop from the working yarn through the two stitches from **back** to **front**, knitting them together as if they were one stitch (**one stitch made**).

BACK

To begin, open the first 15 loops of Black by cutting the centers to create a longer length for sewing.

Beginning at the top edge, cast on 8 loops.

Row 1: Working from **right** to **left**, increase in the first stitch, knit the next 6 stitches, increase in the last stitch: 10 stitches.

Row 2: Working from **left** to **right**, increase in the first stitch, knit the next 8 stitches, increase in the last stitch: 12 stitches.

Row 3: Working from **right** to **left**, increase in the first stitch, knit the next 10 stitches, increase in the last stitch: 14 stitches.

Row 4: Working from **left** to **right**, increase in the first stitch, knit the next 12 stitches, increase in the last stitch: 16 stitches.

Row 5: Working from **right** to **left**, increase in the first stitch, knit the next 14 stitches, increase in the last stitch: 18 stitches.

Row 6: Working from **left** to **right**, increase in the first stitch, knit the next 16 stitches, increase in the last stitch: 20 stitches.

Row 7: Working from **right** to **left**, increase in the first stitch, knit the next 18 stitches, increase in the last stitch: 22 stitches.

Row 8: Working from **left** to **right**, knit each stitch across.

Row 9: Working from **right** to **left**, knit each stitch across.

Rows 10-17: Repeat Rows 8 and 9, 4 times.

Row 18: Working from **left** to **right**, knit the first 2 stitches together **(left over right)**, knit the next 18 stitches, knit the last 2 stitches together **(right over left)**: 20 stitches.

Row 19: Working from **right** to **left**, knit the first 2 stitches together **(right over left)**, knit the next 16 stitches, knit the last 2 stitches together **(left over right)**: 18 stitches.

Row 20: Working from **left** to **right**, knit the first 2 stitches together **(left over right)**, knit the next 14 stitches, knit the last 2 stitches together **(right over left)**: 16 stitches.

Working from **left** to **right**, bind off all stitches.

Cut the yarn 15 loops **past** the last stitch. Cut the loops open so you will have a long tail.

FRONT

To begin, open the first loop of Black by cutting the center to create a longer length for weaving in the end.

With the **right** side of the Back facing and working from **left** to **right** across the cast on edge (at top), pick up 1 stitch **between** each stitch of cast on edge: 7 stitches.

Row 1: Working from **right** to **left**, increase in the first stitch, knit the next 5 stitches, increase in the last stitch: 9 stitches.

Row 2: Working from **left** to **right**, increase in the first stitch, knit the next 7 stitches, increase in the last stitch: 11 stitches.

Note: When instructed to cut a color, cut the working yarn one loop **past** the last stitch; cut the center of the loop open.

Row 3: Working from **right** to **left**, increase in the first stitch, knit the next stitch, cut Black and join Cream; knit the next 7 stitches, cut Cream and join Black; knit the next stitch, increase in the last stitch: 13 stitches.

Row 4: Working from **left** to **right**, increase in the first stitch, knit the next stitch, cut Black and join Cream; knit the next 9 stitches, cut Cream and join Black; knit the next stitch, increase in the last stitch: 15 stitches.

Row 5: Working from **right** to **left**, increase in the first stitch, knit the next 2 stitches, cut Black and join Cream; knit the next 9 stitches, cut Cream and join Black; knit the next 2 stitches, increase in the last stitch: 17 stitches.

Row 6: Working from **left** to **right**, increase in the first stitch, knit the next 3 stitches, cut Black and join Cream; knit the next 9 stitches, cut Cream and join Black; knit the next 3 stitches, increase in the last stitch: 19 stitches.

Row 7: Working from **right** to **left**, increase in the first stitch, knit the next 4 stitches, cut Black and join Cream; knit the next 9 stitches, cut Cream and join Black; knit the next 4 stitches, increase in the last stitch: 21 stitches.

Row 8: Working from **left** to **right**, knit the first 6 stitches, cut Black and join Cream; knit the next 9 stitches, cut Cream and join Black; knit the last 6 stitches.

Row 9: Working from **right** to **left**, knit the first 5 stitches, cut Black and join Cream; knit the next 11 stitches, cut Cream and join Black; knit the last 5 stitches.

Row 10: Working from **left** to **right**, knit the first 5 stitches, cut Black and join Cream; knit the next 11 stitches, cut Cream and join Black; knit the last 5 stitches.

Row 11: Repeat Row 9.

Row 12: Working from **left** to **right**, knit the first 4 stitches, cut Black and join Cream; knit the next 13 stitches, cut Cream and join Black; knit the last 4 stitches.

Row 13: Working from **right** to **left**, knit the first 4 stitches, cut Black and join Cream; knit the next 13 stitches, cut Cream and join Black; knit the last 4 stitches.

Rows 14-16: Repeat Rows 12 and 13 once, then repeat Row 12 once **more**.

Row 17: Repeat Row 9.

Row 18: Working from **left** to **right**, knit the first 2 stitches together (**left over right**), knit the next 4 stitches, cut Black and join Cream; knit the next 9 stitches, cut Cream and join Black; knit the next 4 stitches, knit the last 2 stitches together (**right over left**): 19 stitches.

Row 19: Working from **right** to **left**, knit the first 2 stitches together (**right over left**), knit the next 15 stitches, knit the last 2 stitches together (**left over right**): 17 stitches.

Row 20: Working from **left** to **right**, knit the first 2 stitches together (**left over right**), knit the next 13 stitches, knit the last 2 stitches together (**right over left**): 15 stitches.

Joining: Bring bound off edge of Back up to meet the stitches left on Row 20 of the Front so the **wrong** sides are together. Pull each stitch of Row 20 through the bound off stitches on the Back. Then, working from **left** to **right**, bind off all stitches.

Cut the yarn 3 loops **past** the last stitch. Open the loops by cutting the centers to create a longer length for weaving in the tail.

Bring the long tail through the remaining stitch.

With Orange, cut open the centers of 10 loops to create a long strand. With yarn or tapestry needle and using satin stitch *(Fig. 1)*, add beak, using photo as a guide for placement.

With Black, cut open the centers of 6 loops to create a long strand. With yarn or tapestry needle, add French knot eyes *(Fig. 2)*, using photo as a guide for placement.

Fig. 2

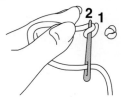

Fig. 1

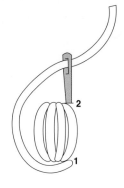

Thread yarn or tapestry needle with long end at base of piece. Sew side seam.

Thread yarn or tapestry needle with long end at top of piece. Sew remaining side seam, stuffing Body lightly with polyester fiberfill before closing.

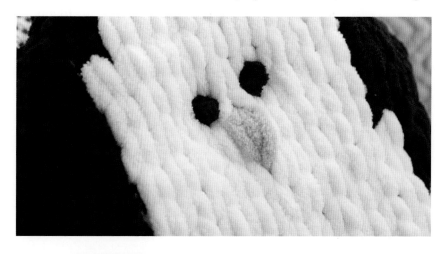

FEET

To begin, open the first 2 loops of Orange by cutting the centers to create a longer length for tying and weaving in the end.

Cast on 6 loops. Tie a knot after the 7th loop to create a ring (between the 6th and 7th loops). **(SEE PHOTO ON PAGE 29)**

Round 1: Working from **right** to **left (now and throughout)**, knit each stitch around: 6 stitches.

Note: Place a split-ring marker around the first stitch of each round to indicate the beginning of the round. Move the marker at the beginning of each round. Remove the marker when it's no longer needed.

Round 2: (Knit the next stitch, increase in the next stitch) 3 times: 9 stitches.

Round 3: Working from **right** to **left**, (knit the next 2 stitches, increase in the next stitch) 3 times: 12 stitches.

Round 4: (Knit the next 3 stitches, increase in the next stitch) 3 times: 15 stitches.

Cut the yarn 8 loops **past** the last stitch. Open the loops by cutting the centers to create a longer length for sewing and weaving in the tail.

Working from **right** to **left**, with end at **wrong** side and beginning with the last stitch of Round 4, bind off all stitches.

Bring the long tail from **back** to **front** through the remaining stitch.

Flatten the piece. Thread your yarn or tapestry needle with the long tail and sew the bind off round together.

Using photo as a guide for placement, sew cast on edge to base of pillow.

Sleep Sack

■□□□ **BASIC**

Nap time has never been so cozy and fashionable. Make this sweet sleep sack in a jiffy with this loopy yarn.

Approximate Finished Size:
12½" wide x 44" long (32 cm x 112 cm) (laying flat)

SHOPPING LIST
Yarn (Jumbo Weight)
[6.4 ounces, 18 yards
(180 grams, 16 meters) per skein]:
☐ 2 skeins

Additional Supplies
☐ Scissors
☐ 1¾" (44 mm) Toggle buttons - 6
☐ Large eye tapestry or yarn needle
☐ Sewing needle and thread

*Please review General Instructions,
pages 52-63, before beginning Sleep Sack.*

TECHNIQUES USED

CABLE 2 LEFT *(abbreviated C2L)* (uses next 2 stitches)
Cross the **next** stitch to the **left** in **front** of the following stitch, then knit the stitches in working order.

CABLE 2 RIGHT *(abbreviated C2R)* (uses next 2 stitches)
Cross the **next** stitch to the **right** in **front** of the following stitch, then knit the stitches in working order.

INSTRUCTIONS

To begin, open the first 6 loops by cutting the centers to create a longer length for sewing the hood seam.

Cast on 18 loops.

Row 1: Working from **right** to **left**, knit the first 8 stitches, work C2L, knit the last 8 stitches.

Row 2: Working from **left** to **right,** knit the first 7 stitches, work C2L, work C2R, knit the last 7 stitches.

Row 3: Working from **right** to **left**, knit the first 6 stitches, work C2R, knit the next 2 stitches, work C2L, knit the last 6 stitches.

Row 4: Working from **left** to **right,** knit the first 5 stitches, work C2L, knit the next 4 stitches, work C2R, knit the last 5 stitches.

Row 5: Working from **right** to **left**, knit the first 5 stitches, work C2L, knit the next 4 stitches, work C2R, knit the last 5 stitches.

Row 6: Working from **left** to **right,** knit the first 6 stitches, work C2R, knit the next 2 stitches, work C2L, knit the last 6 stitches.

Row 7: Working from **right** to **left**, knit the first 7 stitches, work C2L, work C2R, knit the last 7 stitches.

Row 8: Working from **left** to **right,** knit the first 8 stitches, work C2L, knit the last 8 stitches.

Row 9: Working from **right** to **left**, knit the first 7 stitches, work C2R, work C2L, knit the last 7 stitches.

Row 10: Working from **left** to **right,** knit the first 6 stitches, work C2L, knit the next 2 stitches, work C2R, knit the last 6 stitches.

Row 11: Working from **right** to **left**, knit the first 5 stitches, work C2R, knit the next 4 stitches, work C2L, knit the last 5 stitches.

Row 12: Working from **left** to **right,** knit the first 5 stitches, work C2R, knit the next 4 stitches, work C2L, knit the last 5 stitches.

Row 13: Working from **right** to **left**, knit the first 6 stitches, work C2L, knit the next 2 stitches, work C2R, knit the last 6 stitches.

Row 14: Working from **left** to **right,** knit the first 7 stitches, work C2R, work C2L, knit the last 7 stitches.

Rows 15-50: Repeat Rows 1-14 twice, then repeat Rows 1-8 once **more**.

Cut the yarn 3 loops **past** the last stitch. Open the loops by cutting the centers to create a longer length for weaving in the end.

Bind off all stitches from **left** to **right**.

Thread yarn needle with beginning end and sew cast on row together to form hood.

Using sewing needle and thread, sew buttons onto each side and button through the knit stitches.

General Instructions

Yarn Weight Symbol & Names	SUPER FINE 1	FINE 2	LIGHT 3	MEDIUM 4	BULKY 5	SUPER BULKY 6	JUMBO 7
Type of Yarns in Category	Sock, Fingering, Baby	Sport, Baby	DK, Light Worsted	Worsted, Afghan, Aran	Chunky, Craft, Rug	Bulky, Roving	Jumbo, Roving

■□□□ BASIC	Projects using basic stitches. May include basic increases and decreases.
■■□□ EASY	Projects may include simple stitch patterns, color work, and/or shaping.
■■■□ INTERMEDIATE	Projects may include involved stitch patterns, color work, and/or shaping.
■■■■ COMPLEX	Projects may include complex stitch patterns, color work, and/or shaping using a variety of techniques and stitches simultaneously.

COMMON TERMINOLOGY/DEFINITIONS

Cast on — the amount of loops used to begin a project

Working yarn — the yarn that is coming from the ball (consists of loops)

Stitch — the active loops forming the project

Knit (K) — with the working yarn in the **back**, pass the next loop on the working yarn from **back** to **front** through the next stitch

Purl (P) — with the working yarn in the **front**, pass the working yarn from **front** to **back** through the next stitch

Bind off — securing the stitch(es) so the piece doesn't unravel; it can be used within a pattern and will be used on the last row or round to finish

Cable — crossing loops as specified to create a twisted look in the work

Working in the round — each round is made in a circular motion instead of back and forth in rows

Knit 2 Together (K2 tog) — making one stitch from 2 stitches by overlapping them as specified and knitting them together

Knit 3 Together (K3 tog) — making one stitch from 3 stitches by overlapping them as specified and knitting them together

★ — work instructions following ★ as many **more** times as indicated in addition to the first time

BASICS

Cast On

Open the first loop by cutting the center to create a longer length for sewing or weaving in the end. **(PHOTO A)**

With the long end to the **left**, count the number of loops to cast on as given in the individual instructions. Begin your first row in this stitch (loop) **(PHOTO B)**

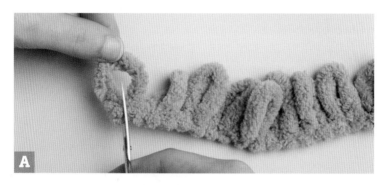

Knit

With the working yarn in the **back**, pass the next unworked loop from **back** to **front** through the next stitch (loop) of the previous row/round (or of the cast on). **(PHOTO C)**

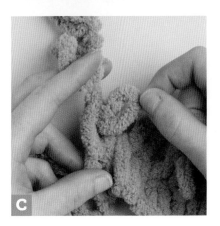

Purl

With the working yarn in the **front**, pass the next unworked loop from **front** to **back** through the next stitch (loop) of the previous row/round (or of the cast on). **(PHOTO D)**

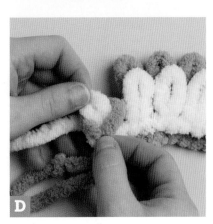

Joining a New Skein *or* Changing Colors

Cut the last loop of the first skein or previous color. **(PHOTO E)**

Cut the first loop of the new skein and knot the 2 ready loops as close as you can get them. **(PHOTO F)**

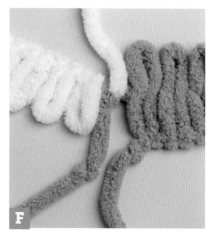

Binding Off

After your last row or round, cut the working yarn 2 loops **past** the last stitch **or** as specified in the individual instructions. **(PHOTO G)**

Cut open the loops so you will have a long tail.

Beginning with the first stitch (loop) at the edge **OPPOSITE** the long tail **or** the stitch specified in the individual instructions, pull up the second stitch through the first stitch (or the stitch specified) from **back** to **front**. You have bound off the first stitch. **(PHOTO H)**

Pull the next stitch through the current stitch from **back** to **front**, and repeat this step until each stitch has been bound off and only one stitch remains.
(PHOTOS I & J)

Bring the long tail completely through the remaining stitch.
(PHOTO K)

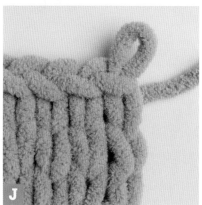

STITCHES & TECHNIQUES

Increase (uses the next stitch)

With the yarn in the **back,** pass the next 2 loops from the working yarn from **back** to **front** through the stitch indicated **(2 stitches made).**
(PHOTOS L and M)

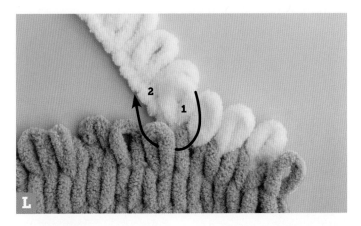

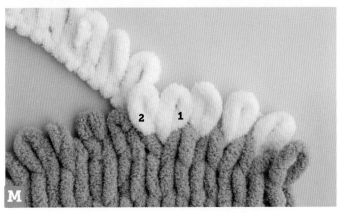

Decreases

KNIT 2 STITCHES TOGETHER (uses the next 2 stitches)
Cross the next 2 stitches as indicated (**right over left** *OR* **left over right**), then pass the next loop from the working yarn through the 2 stitches from **back** to **front**, knitting them together as if they were one stitch **(one stitch made). (PHOTOS N and O)**

right over left

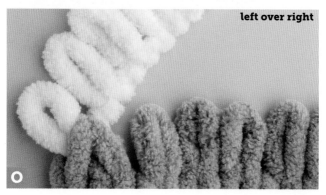

left over right

KNIT 3 STITCHES TOGETHER

(uses the next 3 stitches)

Hold the next stitch **behind** the second stitch and the third stitch **behind** the first stitch, then pass the next loop from the working yarn through all 3 stitches from **back** to **front**, knitting them together as if they were one stitch **(one stitch made). (PHOTO P)**

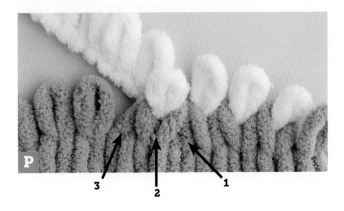

Cables

CABLE 2 LEFT
(abbreviated C2L)
(uses the next 2 stitches)
Cross the **next** stitch to the **left** in **front** of the following stitch, then knit the stitches in working order. **(PHOTO Q)**

CABLE 2 RIGHT
(abbreviated C2R)
(uses the next 2 stitches)
Cross the **next** stitch to the **right** in **front** of the following stitch, then knit the stitches in working order. **(PHOTO R)**

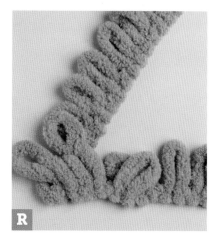

Pulling up *or* Picking up Loops *or* Stitches

Pass the next loop from the working yarn from **back** to **front** (or as specified) under **both** loops of bound off stitch or in the end of a row. **(PHOTOS S and T)**

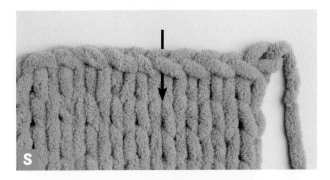

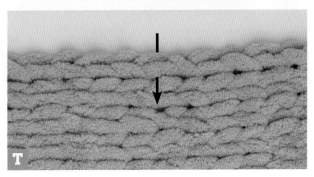

We have made every effort to ensure that these instructions are accurate and complete. We cannot, however, be responsible for human error, typographical mistakes, or variations in individual work.

Production Team: Instructional/Technical Editor - Linda A. Daley; Senior Graphic Artist - Lora Puls; Photo Stylist - Lori Wenger; and Photographer - Jason Masters.

Made in U.S.A.